My Dogs and Guns

Books by John Graves

Goodbye to a River

The Water Hustlers
(with T. H. Watkins and Robert H. Boyle)

Hard Scrabble

The Last Running

Texas Heartland

From a Limestone Ledge

Blue and Some Other Dogs

Self-Portrait, with Birds

A John Graves Reader

John Graves and the Making of
Goodbye to a River

Texas Rivers

Myself and Strangers

My Dogs and Guns

My Dogs and Guns

Two Memoirs, One Beloved Writer

John Graves

Skyhorse Publishing

Skyhorse Publishing books may be purchased in bulk at special discounts for sales promotion, corporate gifts, fund-raising, or educational purposes. Special editions can also be created to specifications. For details, contact the Special Sales Department, Skyhorse Publishing, 307 West 36th Street, 11th Floor, New York, NY 10018 or info@skyhorsepublishing.com.

Skyhorse˚ and Skyhorse Publishing˚ are registered trademarks of Skyhorse Publishing, Inc.˚, a Delaware corporation.

Visit our website at www.skyhorsepublishing.com.

10 9 8 7 6 5 4 3 2 1

Library of Congress Cataloging-in-Publication Data
Graves, John, 1920-
My dogs and guns I John Graves.
p. em.
ISBN-13: 978-1-60239-029-4 (alk. paper)
ISBN-10: 1-60239-029-0 (alk. paper)
1. Graves, John, 1920- 2. Authors, American-
20th century-Biography. 3. Human-animal relationshipsTexas-
Anecdotes. 4. Firearms-Collectors and collecting.
I. Title.
PS3557.R2867Z78 2007
813'.54-dc22
2007003632

Cover design by Adam Bozarth
Cover photos © John Graves

Print ISBN: 978-1-63450-291-7
Ebook ISBN: 978-1-62636-932-0

Printed in the United States of America

Table of Contents

Preface

Versions of the two sections of this book were published nearly twenty years apart as articles in *Texas Monthly* magazine, my chief down-home outlet over time for such work. Despite their variation in vintage, though, the pieces have much in common, which is why my friend Nick Lyons thought of setting them side by side as more or less a unit, and convinced me to undertake the task of adjusting them for that purpose.

This turned out to be a pretty easy job after I determined that I liked both pieces as they stood, and therefore discarded the idea of editing them into a single flowing narrative. I made a few little alterations in the original texts because I'm one of those unfortunate authors who can't look at their own writing in print without wanting to improve it. But other changes, all brief, were needed to avoid repetition or sometimes to clarify connections.

I suppose most persons afflicted with the writing disease who reach an advanced age, as I inexplicably have, look back sometimes on their lifetime production of published matter (pretty sparse, mine has been) in hope of seeing signs of great improvement along the way. So to find two pieces of one's work, widely differing in age, that exhibit so much kinship is . . . well, daunting in a way.

Yet one also has to confront one's own personal self as reflected in one's work, and it is clear to me now that the things I principally cared about, during the period forty or fifty years ago when I was still finding my voice as a writer, are still chiefly the things that move me most—land and water and plants and wild or tame creatures and the ways in which they all connect, along with the kinds of people who have been and still are close to them in one way or another, whether as frontiersmen, hunter-fishermen, birdwatchers, farmers, ranchers, or whatever. And as a writer I have dealt with these things and these human beings chiefly in regional though I hope not provincial terms.

Such rural concerns are of course a long way from the preoccupation with tangled human relationships and dramatic events that has inspired and shaped many of our best writers' efforts. When younger I misspent much time and effort trying to deal with such matters too, but without great joy or success. My focus, it seems, belonged elsewhere.

So be it. Here are some more of the subjects to which this elsewhere focus has led me . . .

John Graves
2006

PART ONE

———

Blue and Some Other Dogs
(1977)

One cool still night last March, when the bitterest winter in decades was starting to slack its grip and the first few chuck-will's-widows were whistling tentative claims to nest territories, the best dog I ever owned simply disappeared. Dogs do disappear, of course. But not usually dogs like Blue or under conditions like ours here in the North Texas cedar hills.

A crossbred Basque-Australian sheepdog, he had spent his whole ten years of life on two North Texas country places and had seldom left the vicinity of the house at either of them without human company since the age of two or less, when his Basque mother was still alive and we also had a lame and anarchic old dachshund that liked to tempt the two of them out roaming after armadillos and feral cats and raccoons and other varmints. This happened usually at night when we had neglected to bring the dachshund into the house, or he had tricked his way outside by faking a call of nature or pushing open an unlatched screen door. The dachshund, named Watty (it started out as Cacahuate, or Peanut), had a very good nose and the sheep dogs didn't, and having located quarry for them he would scream loud sycophantic applause as they pursued it and attacked, sometimes mustering the courage to run in and bite an exposed hind leg while the aggressive mother and son kept the front part angrily busy.

It was fairly gory at times, nor was I that much at war with varmints except periodically with specimens that had developed a taste for chickens or garden crops. But the main problem was the wandering itself, which sometimes took them far from home and onto other property. In the country roaming dogs were and are an abomination, usually in time becoming destructive varmints themselves, large ones that often die from rifle bullets or buckshot or poison bait, well enough deserved. Few people have lived functionally on the land without having to worry sooner or later about such raiders, and the experience makes them jumpy about their own dogs' habits.

To cope, you can chain or pen your dogs when they aren't with you, or you can teach them to stay at home. While I favor the latter approach, with three canines on hand and one of them a perverse and uncontrollable old house pet too entwined with my own past and with the family to get rid of, it was often hard to make training stick with Pan and Blue. At least it was until the dachshund perished under the wheels of a pickup truck, his presence beneath it unsuspected by the driver and his cranky senile arrogance too great to let him scuttle out of the way when the engine started.

Blue's dam was a brindle-and-white Basque sheep dog from Idaho—of a breed said to be called Pannish, though you can't prove that by me since I have never seen another specimen. Taut and compact and aggressive, she was quick to learn but also quick to spot ways to nudge rules aside or to get out of work she didn't savor. She came to us mature and a bit overdisciplined, and if you tried to teach her a task too roughly she would refuse permanently to have anything to do with it. I ruined her for cow work by whipping her for running a heifer through a new fence for the hell of it, and ever afterward if I started dealing with cattle when she was with me, she would go to heel or disappear. Once while chousing a neighbor's Herefords out of an oat patch toward the spate-ripped fence watergap through which they had invaded it, I looked around for Pan and finally glimpsed her peeking at me slyly from a shin-oak thicket just beyond the field's fringe, hiding there till the risk of being called on for help was past.

Not that she feared cows or anything else that walked—or crawled or flew or swam or for that matter rolled on wheels. She attacked strange dogs like a male and had a contemptuous hatred of snakes that made her bore straight in to grab them and shake them dead, even after she had been bitten twice by rattlers, once badly. After such a bout I had seen her with drops of amber venom rolling down her shoulder, where fangs had struck the thick fine hair but had failed to reach her skin. Occasionally she bit people too—always men, though she was nervous enough around unfamiliar children that we never trusted her alone with them. Women, for her own secret reasons, she liked more or less indiscriminately.

She was a sort of loaded weapon, Pan, and in a town or city there would have been no sense in owning such a dog, unless maybe to patrol fenced grounds at night. But we were living then on a leased tract just beyond the western beerhall fringe of Fort Worth, where drunken irrationals roamed the byways after the honkytonks closed, and I was often away. There, what might otherwise have been her worst traits were actually reassuring. She worshipped my wife Jane, slept beside the bed when I was gone, and would, I am certain, have died in defense of the household with the same driven ferocity she showed in combat with wild things.

A big boar coon nearly got her one January night, before she had Blue as a cohort. The old dachshund Watty had sicced her on it by the barn, where it had come for a bantam supper, and by the time I had waked to the noise and pulled on pants and located a flashlight, the fight had rolled down to the creek and Pan's chopping yap had suddenly stilled, though Watty was still squalling hard. When I got there and shone the light on a commotion in the water, all that showed was the coon's solemn face and shoulders. Astraddle Pan's neck with an ear clutched in each hand, he was quite competently holding her head down despite her mightiest struggles. Big bubbles rolled up as I watched, with Watty dancing still uproarious beside me on good firm land. Grabbing up a stick I waded into the frigid chest-deep pool, whacked the coon out of his saddle, declined his offer to climb me in retaliation, and sent him swimming for the other bank. But by then Pan was unconscious, and on shore I shook and pumped the better part of a gallon of water out of her before she started to wheeze and cough.

Which didn't keep her from assaulting the very next coon her brave, small, black friend sniffed out, though she never followed another one into water. She was not too rash to learn what an impossibility was.

We had a plague of feral housecats in that place, strayed outward from the city or dumped along the roads by the kind of people who do that sort of thing, and a huge tom one evening gave Watty his comeuppance. After a notable scrap with Pan, the tom decided to leave when I arrived, but she grabbed him by the tail as he fled. At this point old Watty, thinking in dim light that the customary face-to-face squabble was still in progress and gaining from my arrival some of the courage that the cat had lost, dashed in for a furtive chomp and was received in a loving, tight, clawed embrace with sharp teeth in its middle. His dismay was piercingly loud and he bore those scars for the rest of his life. The tomcat got away.

If my less than objective interest in these violent matters is evident, I have the grace to be a bit ashamed, but not very. I have had close friends among the hound-dog men whose main pleasure in life has lain in fomenting such pursuits and brawls, and some of them have been quite gentle people. That is to say I have never been of the school that believes hunting per se makes worse brutes of men than they already are. I seldom encouraged those home-ground uproars between my own dogs and varmints until later, when Pan was gone and Blue had constituted himself Protector of Garden and Poultry. The toll of wildlife actually killed over the years was light, reaching a mild peak during the brief period after Blue was full grown and before Pan died, when they hunted and fought as a skillful team. Most chases would end with a treeing and I would call the dogs home with no real damage having been done on either side. But Man the Hunter's association with dogs is very very longstanding, and any man who can watch a slashing battle between his own dogs and something wild and tough, when it does occur, without feeling a flow of the old visceral, reckless joy, is either quite skilled at suppressing his emotions or more different from me than I think most men are.

There being of course the additional, perhaps more cogent fact that in the country varmints around the house, garden, barn, and chicken yard are bad news, and the best help in keeping them away is aggressive dogs.

Unable to find any males of Pan's breed in this region, we mated her with one of those more numerous herding dogs, similar in build and coat but colored white and black-speckled gray, known commonly as Australian Blue Heelers or just Australians. Three of the resulting pups had her coloration and the fourth was Blue, marked like his sire but with less speckling and no trace of the blue "glass" or "china" tinge that many, perhaps most Australians have in one or both eyes, sometimes as only a queer pale blaze on an iris. When the time came to choose, we picked him to keep, and as a result he turned out to be a far different sort of grown dog than he would have been if we had given him away.

For Pan was an impossibly capricious, domineering mother, neurotic in her protectiveness but punitive toward the pups to the point of drawing blood when they annoyed her, which was often. The rest got out from under at six or eight weeks of age, but Blue had to stay and take it, and kept on taking it until Pan died—run over while nudging at the rule against chasing cars. Even after Blue had reached full size—at seventy-five pounds half again larger than either Pan or his sire—he had to be always on the watch for her unforeseeable fits of displeasure.

I used to wish he would round on her and whip her hard once and for all, but he never did. Instead he developed the knack of turning clownish at a moment's notice, reverting to ingratiating puppy tricks to deflect the edge of her wrath. He would run around in senseless circles yapping, would roll on his back with his feet wiggling in the air, all the while grinning—crinkling his eyes and turning up the corners of his mouth and lolling his tongue out over genially bared teeth. At these times he was a travesty of all mashed-down human beings who have had to clown to survive, like certain black barbershop shoeshine "boys," some of them sixty years old, that I remembered from my youth.

These tricks worked well enough on Pan that they became a permanent part of the way Blue was, and he brought them to his relationships with people, mainly me, where they worked also. It was quite hard to stay angry at a large strong dog, no matter what he had just done, who had his bobtailed butt in the air and his head along his forelegs on the ground and his eyes skewed sidewise at you as he smiled a wide, mad, minstrel-show smile. If I did manage to stay angry despite all, he would most often panic and flee to his hideout beneath the pickup's greasy differential—which may have been another effect of Pan's gentle motherliness or may just have been Australian; they are sensitive beasts, easily cowed, that require light handling. For the most part all that Blue did need was light handling, for he wanted immensely to please and was the easiest dog to train in standard matters of behavior that I had ever dealt with. Hating cats, for instance, he listened to one brief lecture concerning a kitten just bought by our small daughters for twenty-five cents at a church benefit sale, and not only tolerated her thereafter but became her staunchest friend, except perhaps in the matter of tomcats she favored when older, which he kept chasing off. And he learned things like heeling in a couple of hours of casual coaching.

Which harks back to my description of him as the best dog I had ever owned. He was. But it is needful at this point to confess that that is not saying much. Nearly all the dogs I had possessed before Pan and Blue and Watty were pets I had as a boy in Fort Worth, a succession of fox terriers and curs and whatnot that I babied, teased, cajoled, overfed, and generally spoiled in the anthropomorphic manner of kids everywhere. Most perished young, crushed by cars, and were mourned with tears and soon replaced by others much like them in undisciplined worthlessness. In those years I consumed with enthusiasm Jack London's dog books and other less sinewy stuff like the works of Albert Payson Terhune, with their tales of noble and useful canines, but somehow I was never vouchsafed the ownership of anything that faintly resembled Lad or Buck or White Fang. The best of the lot was a brown-and-white mongrel stray that showed up already gray-chopped, with beautiful manners and training, but he liked adults better than children and stayed with my father when he could.

The worst but most loved was an oversized Scotty named Roderick Dhu, or Roddy, who when I was twelve of thirteen or so used to accompany me and a friend on cumbersome hunting and camping expeditions to the Trinity West Fork bottomland beyond the city's edge, our wilderness. Roddy had huge negative willpower and when tired or hot would often sit down and refuse to move another inch. Hence from more than one of those outings I came hiking back out of the bottom burdened with not only a Confederate bedroll full of cooking and camping gear, a .22 rifle, a Bowie knife, an ax, and other such impediments, but also with thirty-five deadweight pounds of warm dog. I guess I should have seen it as a blessing when Roddy got run over by a Model A Ford, but I didn't.

The friend's dog in contrast was a quick bright feist called Buckshot, destined to survive not only our childhood but our college years, World War Two, and nearly a decade longer, dying ultimately, my friend swears, at the age of twenty-two. A canine wraith toward the end, nearly blind and grayed all over and shrunken, he would lie in corners and dream twitching of old possums and rabbits we had harried through the bottomland's ferns and poison ivy, thumping his tail on the floor when human movement was near if he chanced to be awake.

With this background, although I knew about useful dogs from reading, from having friends and relatives with good pointers and setters, and from watching excellent herding dogs as a teenager when I had summer jobs in the country, I managed to arrive at adult years with a fairly intact urban, middle-class, sentimental ideal of the Nice Dog, a clean-cut fellow that obeyed a few essential commands, was loyal and gentle with his masters, and refrained from "bad" behavior as defined by those masters. I had never had one and knew it, and the first dog I owned after years of unsettled, often wandering existence was the dachshund Watty, who was emphatically not one either.

He started out all right, intelligent and affectionate and as willing to learn as dachshunds ever are, and with the nose he had he made a fair retriever, albeit hard-mouthed with shot birds and inclined to mangle them a bit before reluctantly giving them up. He was pleasant company, too, and we had some fine times together, including the canoe trip I wrote about in my book *Goodbye to a River*. But his temper started souring when Jane and I married, grew vile when children came, and was ultimately ruined by a paralyzing back injury, never completely rectified, and by much sympathetic spoiling along the way. As an old cripple, a stage that lasted at least five years, he snarled, bit, disobeyed, stank constantly and broke wind to compound it, yowled and barked for his supper in the kitchen for two hours before feeding time, subverted the good sheep dogs' training, and was in general the horrid though small-scale antithesis of a Nice Dog. And yet in replication of my childhood self I loved him, and buried him wrapped in a feed sack under a flat slab of limestone with his name scratched deep upon it.

While for Blue, than whom I doubt I'll ever have a Nicer Dog even if perhaps one more useful, there is no marker at all because there is no grave on which to put one. . . .

I do think Watty knocked out of me most of my residual kid sentimentality about dogs in general—he along with rural living where realism has been forced upon me by predatory packs of canines and the owner-

ship of Pan and Blue with their strong thrust and poten-
tial, never fully attained—to the point that I'm certain I
will never put up with an unmanageable dog again. I
remember one time of sharp realization during the
second summer after we bought this cedar-hill place,
before we lived here any part of the year or had Pan and
Blue or even used the land for grazing livestock. That
spring, after the dachshund had been thrown from the
pickup's seat when I had to jam the brakes on in traffic,
I carried him partly paralyzed to the vet in Fort Worth,
a friend, who advised me frankly that the smart thing
would be to put him down. But he added that he had
always wanted to try to heal one of those tricky dachshund spines, and that if I would go along with him he
would charge me only his actual costs. Though by that
time Watty was already grumpy and snappish and very
little pleasure to have around, sentimentality of course
triumphed over smart. "Actual costs" soon headed sky-
ward, and even now in far costlier times I can grunt
when I think of them.

During the cool months at that time I was teaching college classes in Fort Worth, but that second summer I started some of the endless construction that has marked our tenure of the country land. I was in and out every day or so with loads of lumber and cement and other materials, and paused sometimes to talk with a pleasant countryman who lived on the road I used. He had a heterogeneous little troop of dogs around the yard, some useful and some just there, their ringleader a small white cur with pricked ears and red-rimmed eyes who chased cars and was very noisy, but was prized by the man's children and had the redeeming trait of being, quote, hell at finding rattlesnakes.

One morning as I drove in, this dog was sitting upright under a live oak fifty yards or so from the house, with his head held oddly high and askew. He had found one rattler too many. His eyes were nearly shut and on the side of his neck was a lump about the size of his head. Nor did he acknowledge my passing with so much as a stifled yap.

Thinking perhaps they didn't know, I stopped by the house.

"Yes," said my friend. "He run onto a big one up by the tank yesterday evening and by the time I got there with a hoe it had done popped him good."

"Did you do anything for him?"

"Well, we put some coal oil on it," he said. "I was going to cut it open but there's all them veins and things. You know, they say if a rattler hits a dog on the body he's a goner, but if it's the head he'll get all right. You reckon the neck's the head?"

I said I hoped so, and for days as I passed in and out I watched the little dog under his oak tree, from which he did not stir, and checked with the family about him. They were not at all indifferent; he was a main focus of concern and they kept fresh food and water by him. The neck swelled up and broke open, purging terrible fluids. After this happened he seemed to feel better and even ate a little, but then one morning he was dead. Everyone including me was sad that he had lost his fight to live, and the children held a funeral for him, with bouquets of wild prairie pinks.

And such was my changing view that this seemed somehow to make more healthy sense than all that cash I was ramming into a spoiled irascible dachshund's problematic cure . . .

Really good country dogs are something else, and are often treated like family members and worried over as much when sick or hurt. This is not sentimentality but hard realism, because such dogs are worth fretting about in pragmatic terms. There aren't all that many of them. As excellent dogs always have, they come mainly from ruthless culling of promising litters and from close careful training, and most belong to genuine stockmen with lots of herding work to do. These owners routinely turn down offers of hundreds of dollars for them, if you believe the stories, as you well may after watching a pair of scroungy border collies, in response to a low whistle or a softly spoken command, run a half-mile up a brush-thick pasture to bring back seventy-nine Angora wethers and immobilize them in a fence corner or a pen for shearing, doctoring, worming, or loading into a trailer, all while their master picks his teeth.

Blue wasn't that kind of dog or anywhere near it, nor was there much chance to develop such talent on a place like ours, where the resident cows and goats are fairly placid and few problems emerge in handling them that can't be solved with a little patience and a rattling bucket of feed. For that matter, I don't know nearly enough about the training of such dogs to have helped him become one. A livestock buyer and trader whom I knew and liked and who had superb dogs himself, did once tell me, after watching Blue try to help us one morning, that if I'd lend my Australian/Basque clown to him for six months he might be able to "make a dog out of him." I was grateful and tempted and thought it over, but in the end declined, partly because I mistrusted what a long spell of training by a stranger might do to that queer, one-man, nervous streak in Blue, but mainly because I didn't know what I'd do with such a dog if I had him, in our miniature and unstrenuous livestock operations. His skills would rust unused, and the fact I had to confront was that I didn't deserve a dog like that.

What Blue amounted to, I guess, was a country Nice Dog, which in terms of utility is a notable cut above the same thing in the city. These rural equivalents stay strictly at home, announce visitors, keep varmints and marauding dogs and unidentified nocturnal boogers away, cope with snakes (Blue, after one bad fanging that nearly killed him, abandoned his mother's tactics of headlong assault and would circle a snake raising hell until I came to kill it, or to call him off if it was harmless), watch over one's younger children, and are middling to good help at shoving beasts through a loading chute or from one pen to another, but less help in pastures where the aiming point may be a single gate in a long stretch of fence and judgment is required.

Some learn simple daily herding tasks like bringing in milk cows at evening, though I have observed that much of the time these tasks involve an illusion on the part of the dog and perhaps his owner that he is making cows or goats or sheep do something that actually they have full intention of doing on their own, unforced. Or the whole thing may be for fun, as it was with one old rancher I knew, who had an ancient collie named Babe. When visitors came to sit with the old man on his porch, he would at some point level a puzzled blue glare across the pasture and say in conversational tones, "I declare, Babe, it looks like that old mare has busted out of the corral again. Maybe you better bring her in." And Babe would rise and go do as he was bidden and the visitors would be much impressed, unless they happened to know that that was the one sole thing he could do and the mare was in on it too.

On the whole, to be honest, Blue was pretty poor at herding even by such relaxed standards—too eager and exuberant and only occasionally certain of what it was we were trying to do. But he was controllable by single words and gestures and like his mother unafraid, and in his later years when I knew his every weakness, such as nipping goats, I could correct mistakes before he made them, so that he was often of some help. He was even more often comic relief, as when a chuted cow turned fighty and loaded him into the trailer instead of he her, or when a young bull, too closely pressed, kicked him into a thick clump of scrub elm, where he landed upside down with his legs still running in the air. When I went over and saw that he wasn't hurt and started laughing at the way he looked, he started laughing too, at least in his own way.

For a sense of humor and of joy was the other side of that puppyish clowning streak which he always retained but which turned less defensive with time. The nervousness that went with it never left either, but grew separate from the clowning, ritualizing itself most often in a weird habit he had of grinning and slobbering and clicking his teeth together when frustrated or perplexed. He regularly did this, for instance, when friends showed up for visits and brought their own dogs along. Knowing he wasn't supposed to attack these as he did strays, Blue was uncertain what else to do with them. So he would circle them stiff-legged, wagging his stub and usually trying to mount them, male or female, small or large, and after being indignantly rebuffed would walk about popping his jaws and dribbling copious saliva. I expect some of those visiting friends thought him a very strange dog indeed, and maybe in truth he was.

He was a bouncing, bristling, loudmouthed watchdog when I was at home, bulkily impressive enough that arriving strangers would most often stay in their cars till I came out to call him off. Unlike Pan, he bore them no real hostility and never bit anyone, though I believe if any person or thing had threatened one of us those big white teeth would have been put to good use. Mainly unfamiliar people disconcerted him and he wanted nothing to do with them, unless I showed myself receptive, at which point he was wont to start nuzzling their legs and hands like a great overgrown pup demanding caresses. Once when the pickup was ailing I left it at a garage in town and mooched a ride home with a friend whose car Blue didn't know. No one in the family was there, and when we drove up to the house there was no sign of a dog, but then I saw him peering furtively around a corner of the porch, much as his mother had eyed me from those shin-oak bushes long before.

With his size, clean markings, silky thick coat, broad head, alert eyes, and usual aspect of grave dignity, he was a handsome creature. Having him along was often an asset with strangers, even if it could turn out to be the opposite if something disturbed him and he started popping his jaws and drooling and grinning that ghastly grin. One day when he was young and we were still living outside Fort Worth, I was apprehended in that city for running a red light, though I had thought to discern no light on at all when I drove through the intersection. I explained this to the arresting officer, a decent type, and together we went back and watched the damned thing cycle through six or eight perfectly sequenced changes from green to yellow to red and back again. Blue watched with us and, somehow attuned to the situation, accepted a pat on the head from the cop with an austere but friendly smile. Against pregnant silence I said with embarrassment that I guessed my eyesight was failing faster than I'd thought, accepted the inevitable summons, and went my disgruntled way.

When I got home that afternoon, Jane said the officer had telephoned. More decent even than I'd known, he had watched the light for a while longer by himself and had finally caught it malfunctioning. He told her I could get the ticket canceled.

She had thought me off in the cedar hills and believed there was a mistake. "Did he have a sheepdog in the back of the pickup?" she asked.

"No, ma'am," replied Blue's till-then secret admirer. "That big beautiful animal was sitting right up on the front seat with him."

We spent a tremendous lot of time together over the years, Blue and I—around the house and barn and pens, wandering on the place, batting about in a pickup (his pickup more than mine in a way, for he spent much of each day in its bed or underneath, even when it was parked by the house), or at farm work in the fields. When young he would follow the tractor around and around as I plowed or harrowed or sowed, but later he learned to sit under a shady tree and watch my progress in comfort, certain I was not escaping from him. Sometimes when he got bored he would bounce out to meet the tractor as it passed and would try to lead it home.

Fond of the whole family and loved by all, he would go along with the girls to swim at the creek or on horseback jaunts across the hills, good protection for them and good company. But he needed a single main focus and I was it, so completely that at times I felt myself under surveillance. No imperfectly latched door escaped his notice if I was indoors and he was out, and he could open one either by shoving or by pulling it with his teeth, as permanent gouge-marks on some of them still testify. Failing to get in, he would ascertain as best he could, by peeking in windows or otherwise, just where I was located inside and then would station himself by the outer wall closest to that spot, even if it put him in the full blast of a January norther.

At one friend's house in the local town that he and I visited often, he would if left outside go through the attached garage to a warped kitchen door at war with its jamb and seldom completely closed. Easing through it, he would traverse the breakfast room and a hall, putting one foot before another in tense slow motion, would slink behind a sofa into the living room, and using concealment as craftily as any old infantryman, would sometimes be lying beside my chair before either I or my friend knew he was there. More usually, though, we would watch his creeping progress while pretending not to notice, and after he got where he was headed I would deliver a loud mock scolding and he would roll on his back and clown, knowing he was home free and wouldn't be booted back outside, as sometimes happened when he had fat ticks acquired at our creek or was stinking from a recent scrap with some polecat.

But there were places he wouldn't go to with me, most notably the bee yard, his first apicultural experience having been his definite last. It had happened one early spring day when I was helping that same friend in town check through a neglected hive somebody had given him. Blue had tagged along, unsuspecting. The hive was all gummed up, its frames and combs stuck together with bridge-wax and propopolis so that we had to tear them loose from one another in order to take them out. And on that chilly day all thirty or forty thousand worker bees were at home and ready to fight. They got under our veils and into our gloves and sleeves and all cracks in our attire, and those that didn't manage entry just rammed their stingers through a couple of layers of cloth. They also found Blue, a prime target for apian rage since bees hate all hairy things, probably out of ancestral recollection of honey-loving bears.

With maybe a hundred of them hung whining in his hair and stinging whenever they found skin, Blue tried to squeeze between my legs for protection and caused me to drop a frame covered with bees, which augmented the assault. Shortly thereafter, torn between mirth and pain, we gave up, slapped the hive back together, and lit out at a run, with Blue thirty yards ahead and clouds of bees flying escort.

After that experience, whenever Blue saw me donning the veil and firing up my smoker, he would head for distant shelter. He did work out a method of revenge, though, which he used for the rest of his life despite scoldings and other discouragements. Finding a place where small numbers of bees were coming for some reason—a spot on the lawn where something sweet had been spilled, perhaps, or a lime-crusted dripping faucet whose flavor in their queer way they liked—he would stalk it with his special tiptoeing slink and then loudly snap bees from the air one by one as they appeared, apparently not much minding the occasional stings he got on his lips and tongue. I suppose I could have broken him of this, but it was a ludicrous thing to watch and for that matter he didn't get many bees in relation to their huge numbers—unlike another bee-keeper friend's Dalmatian, imbued with similar feelings, who used to sit all day directly in front of a hive chomping everything that emerged, and had to be given away.

Maybe Blue considered bees varmints. He took his guardianship of the home premises dead seriously and missed few creatures that invaded the yard and garden. Except for the unfortunate armadillos, which he had learned to crunch, the mortality inflicted was low after Pan's death, as I have said, for most intruders could escape through the net-wire fence that momentarily blocked Blue's pursuit and few of them cared to stay and dispute matters except an occasional big squalling coon. We did have some fine midnight tussles with these, though I suppose I'd better not further sully my kindly aura, if any remains, by going into details. The peak of hostilities came during the time when cantaloupes and roasting ears were coming ripe and were most attractive to coons. I would leave the garden gate open at dark and Blue would go down during the night on patrol. There was sometimes a question as to whether a squad of coons given full license could have done half as much damage to garden crops as the ensuing battles did, but there was no question at all about whether the procedure worked. After only two or three brawls each year, word would spread around canny coondom that large hairy danger lurked in the Graves corn patch and they would come no more, much to Blue's disappointment.

I talked to him quite a bit, for the most part childishly or joshingly as one does talk to beasts, and while I am not idiot enough to think he "understood" any of it beyond a few key words and phrases, he knew my voice's inflections and tones, and by listening took meaning from them if meaning was there to be had, responding with a grin, a sober stare, melting affection, or some communicative panting, according to what seemed right to him. Like most dogs that converse with humans he was a thorough yes type, honoring my every point with agreement. Nice Dogs are ego-boosters, and have been so since the dim red dawn of things.

I could leave him alone and untethered at the place for a couple of days at a time, with dry food in a bucket under shelter and water to be had at the cattle troughs. Neighbors a half-mile away told me that sometimes when the wind was right they could hear him crooning softly wolflike, lonely, but he seemed never to leave the place. When I came back he would be at the yard gate waiting, and as I walked toward the house he would dance beside me, leaping four and five feet straight up in the air in pure and utter celebration, whining and grunting maybe but seldom more, for he saved loud barks for strangers and snakes and varmints and such.

Last winter I slept inside the house instead of on the screen porch we usually shared as night quarters unless, as often, he wanted to be outside on guard. And I hadn't moved back out by that March night when he vanished. He had been sleeping on a horse blanket on a small unscreened side porch facing south, and I had begun to notice that sometimes he would be still abed and pleasantly groggy when I came out at daybreak. He was fattening a bit also, and those eyes were dimmer that once had been able to pick me out of a sidewalk crowd of jostling strangers half a block away in town, and track me as I came toward the car. But now, like mine, his years were piling up. It was a sort of further bond between us.

He ate a full supper that evening and barked back with authority at some coyotes singing across the creek, and in the morning he was gone. I had to drive two counties north that day to pick up some grapevines and had planned to take him along. When he didn't answer my calls I decided he must have a squirrel in the elms and cedars beyond the little house branch, where he would often sit silent and taut for hours staring up at a treed rodent, oblivious to summonings. It was a small sin that I permitted him at his age; if I needed him I could go and search him out and bring him in, for he was never far away. But that day it didn't seem to matter, and I took off without him, certain he'd be at the yard gate when I drove in after lunch, as he had invariably been over the years.

Except that he wasn't. Nor did a tour of his squirrel grounds yield any trace, or careful trudges up and down the branch, or a widening week-long search by myself and Jane and our daughters (whose spring school vacation it used up and utterly ruined), a search that involved every brushpile and crevice we could find within half a mile or more of home, where Blue might have followed some varmint and gotten stuck or bitten in a vein by a rattler just out of its winter's doze and full of rage and venom. We watched for the tight down-spiral of feeding vultures, drove all the county's roads and talked to people who, no, had not seen any dogs like that or even any bitches in heat that might have passed through, recruiting. We ran ads in the local paper and taped notices to the doors of feed stores and groceries, which produced some false hopes that led me up to thirty miles away in vain.

Even his friend the two-bit cat, at intervals for weeks, would sit and mew toward the woods in queer and futile lament.

I ended fairly certain of what I had surmised from the first, that Blue lay dead, from whatever cause, beneath some thick heap of bulldozed brush or in one of those holes, sometimes almost caves, that ground-water had eaten out under the limestone ledges of our hills. For in country as brushy and wrinkled and secret as ours, we couldn't have found all such places round-about, even close.

Or maybe I want to believe this because it has finality.

And maybe he will still turn up, like those long-lost animals you read about in children's books and sometimes in newspaper stories.

No, he won't.

And dogs are nothing but dogs and I know it better than most, and all this worry has been for a queer and nervous old crossbreed that couldn't even herd stock right. Nor was there anything humanly unique about the loss, or about the emptiness that came in the searching's wake, which sooner or later has afflicted all people foolish enough to give an animal space in their lives. But if you are built to be such a fool, you are, and if the animal is to you what Blue was to me the space he leaves empty is big.

It is partly filled for us now by a successor, an Old English pup with much promise—sharp and alert, wildly vigorous but responsive and honest, puppy-clownish but with an underlying gravity that will in time I think prevail. There is nothing nervous about him; he has a sensitivity that could warp in that direction if mishandled, but won't if I can help it. Nor does he show any fear beyond healthy puppy caution, and in the way he looks at cows and goats and listens to people's words I see clearly that he may make a hell of a dog, quite possibly better than Blue. Which is not, as I said, saying much.

But he isn't Blue. In the domed shape of his head under my hand as I sit reading in the evenings I can still feel that broader, silkier head, and through his half-boisterous, half-bashful glad morning hello I still glimpse Blue's clown grin and crazy leaps. I expect such intimate remembrance will last a good long while, for I waited the better part of a lifetime to own a decent dog, and finally had him, and now don't have him any more. And I resolve that when this new one is grown and more or less shaped in his ways, I am going to get another pup to raise beside him, and later maybe a third. Because I don't believe I want to face so big a dose of that sort of emptiness again.

PART TWO

Guns of a Lifetime, with a Few More Tales (2006)

I am not a member of the National Rifle Association, nor do I collect rare firearms, attend gun shows, or subscribe to gun magazines. I am not, in other words, a "gun nut," and in fact can sympathize, if a bit faintly, with the views of those who detest all such weapons and want them regulated. You can't have lived in a large American city for any length of time, as I have, without seeing that such people's opinions may have a certain amount of validity.

But I grew up in a time and a region that almost automatically sparked interest in not only guns but the hunting of birds and beasts, in which pursuits such weapons were and still are central components. Nor did a war experienced in the U. S. Marine Corps and a functional country life during most of the past forty-odd years do anything to hamper the affinity.

This piece of writing stems from a letter I wrote to my wife Jane's and my two daughters, who both now live far from Texas but retain an appreciation of the rural surroundings in which they mainly grew up. And both, for whatever reasons, had expressed specific curiosity about the remembered and varying assortment of firearms accumulated by their male parent during his sojourn in this vale of sorrows, which has now lasted eighty-six years. Neither daughter is a gun enthusiast—they just remembered these weapons, most of which have moved along elsewhere by now, and wanted to know the stories of those that had one.

So here are the stories, with a few extras and detours thrown in as what the Mexicans call pilón, something extra. They are not all "nice" tales in contemporary terms. Political incorrectness, as presently defined, may be perpetrated here and there, though I hope no parts will seem like the maunderings of a Deep South redneck. But if they do, the hell with it. I am too old to fret about such matters.

Pistols

My earliest pistol was a rusted and cylinderless revolver I found in an area, near where I grew up in Fort Worth, that had been the sprawling site of World War One's Camp Bowie. And I recall a battered, nickel-plated .38 of a dubious cheap foreign brand, which had been confiscated from some miscreant in Cuero, Texas, when my very casual Uncle Tommy Graves had been county judge there. He reconfiscated it and gave it to me when I was quite young, but my father got rid of it as soon as he found out that I had it.

Colt .32-caliber semi-automatic, Model 1903. This was one of a couple of antiques in the collection, both deriving from that same ancestral town of Cuero. My grandfather, the first John Alexander Graves, was not at all interested in weaponry, though two of his three sons were avid hunters, mainly of quail, doves, ducks, and such. And their brother, my father, had also hunted with enthusiasm when younger.

Grandpa's main passions, as I remember and was told about them, were for horsemanship, at which he was very adept in a non-cowboy way, having grown up in Missouri, for the Episcopal Church, and for merchandising, in which he also excelled. But he was quite conscious too, like most white Southerners of his time, of his personal honor, which was considerable because he tried to live up to the principles he espoused.

In accordance with a frequent post-Civil-War Southern practice, highly reprehensible by today's standards, he would sometimes make a deal with the local sheriff to take a nonviolent black prisoner off of the county's hands during what remained of the man's sentence, and put him to work at home or in the dry goods store, taking responsibility for his nourishment and shelter and continued local presence.

At one point not long after the turn of the twentieth century, when Grandpa was in his forties, he acquired such a servant and used him at home, chiefly in the yard, garden, and horse lot, the latter holding a couple of high-bred geldings, one of which Grandpa would ride to town and back in the mornings (he always came home for the large midday meal, called dinner in those times) and the other for use in the afternoons, to and from his store. In summer he would be dressed in a white linen suit and Panama hat, and in winter in black with a derby, thus emphasizing the non-cowboy motif. He continued that practice into my own lifetime, after he had sold the store but still rode down to an office and back twice each day. But he did finally start using a Western saddle.

This black man's former employer was a local gambler, who came to the house one day when Grandpa was not present and persuaded or ordered the man to return to the saloon where he plied his cards and dice.

Learning what had happened, Grandpa drove his horse-drawn buggy to the saloon, and because when young he had promised his mother never to enter such an establishment, he called the gambler out onto the board sidewalk. Harsh words ensued, said gambler not being a mild fellow, and Grandpa ended by taking his horsewhip from the buggy and using it until his foe was writhing prostrate on the planks. Then, with the black man aboard, he headed home. But the last thing he heard from the felled gambler was a squawked "Damn you, I'm gonna kill you! You watch!"

Ever realistic, my grandsire went to a hardware store owned by a friend and purchased this pistol, a novelty and something of an anomaly in a time when most personal armament in Texas still consisted of large-bore single-action revolvers. He practiced firing it in the horse lot until he could hit more or less what he was aiming at, and then carried it in a coat pocket for a couple of months or so until he learned that his gambler had left town for good without making any move toward fulfilling his threat.

When Grandpa died in a car wreck at eighty, in the 1930s, this pistol along with other personal items passed to my father in Fort Worth, who never fired it except on one unfortunate occasion in 1947, when I was in graduate school at Columbia University in New York.

A family of south European origins had moved into the house next-door to Mama and Papa's. They had seemed quite decent the one time I had been around them, though they were a bit messy and raucous, and Papa was not happy about this. As it turned out, he had been drinking rather heavily for years, though without ever seeming even tipsy ("Drink all you want to," he had once told me, "but never let it show"), and when our family doctor put him on a newfangled antihistamine for a respiratory problem, its reaction with alcohol set his mind ablaze. One night he took the old .32 out into the front yard and starting shooting it into the upper branches of a hackberry tree, saying to my mother when she came out and protested: "There are Greeks up there and they're laughing at me!"

My father was a man of low-keyed presence and no flamboyance at all, so this was a startling event. I flew home from the East and Papa experienced some hospital time, but he said he was going to quit drinking and he did, cold turkey. The pistol, however, he wanted nothing further to do with, and its ownership passed to me. It must not have been cleaned since Grandpa had fired old-style cartridges in it, with corrosive primers, for its barrel was badly pitted. I had a gunsmith order a new one, which stuck out of the housing a bit farther than the old one had.

Except for a little practice shooting, I've fortunately never had occasion to employ this weapon, though I remember one time when I thought I might have to do so. My first wife and I were driving back home from Albuquerque one early fall across the empty plains of eastern New Mexico (very empty, back then) when we came up out of a dip and saw to our right an old black sedan, upside-down in a cloud of dust and with its wheels still turning. This looked improbable enough to have been staged, so I drove a little past it, took the .32 from the glove compartment, told my wife to drive on if there was trouble, and walked back to the dusty scene, which turned out to be quite genuine. The topsy-turvy jalopy was full of drunk sheep-shearers who were so crammed together that only a couple of them had some bruises and scrapes and cuts. We dropped those two off at a doctor's place in the next town—I forget what town that was—and tooled on homeward with the small weapon that still hadn't claimed any victims.

Colt .45-caliber semi-automatic. The potent sidearm our military developed for use in the Philippines against homicidal Muslim Moros, shades of the present. In the armed forces it had been issued to officers and higher NCOs, though mine was a civilian model. I won it in a poker game aboard a troopship during World War Two, at some point had it adorned with stag-horn grips, and lost it after the war when a thief found and took it from beneath the front seat of my car, where I had unwisely placed it.

During my brief combat time in the Pacific I carried this .45 as well as an issue .30-caliber carbine, but I remember only once when I used the pistol out there. During our first night on the beach at Saipan in June

1944, a very dark night, individual Japanese infiltrators seemed to be everywhere, dropping grenades into people's foxholes, knifing them, and otherwise playing such merry hell that we were all on edge. At one point, in the dimness I saw a form skulking along in the salt shallows just off of the beach, challenged it and received no reply, and cut loose with the .45. What I shot holes in turned out to be not a hostile Asian but a small metal barrel propelled bobbingly by a light breeze, a discovery that made me feel very foolish indeed. But it was that kind of night, and several lost or blundering Americans got killed or wounded by nervous fellow-countrymen.

Colt "Frontier Scout" .22-caliber single-action revolver. This one had the shape and longish barrel of the old gun-fighters' heavier weapon, but it disappeared long ago, either stolen or, more likely, hidden by me in some secret niche of this country house that is now secret from myself also. I had bought it at the instigation of a ranching friend, Tommy Harrison, a rough-hewn ruralist and backward-looker. I liked it very much—simple, safe, comfortable in the hand, and extremely accurate.

Colt .357 Magnum revolver. I bought this pistol (why?) in the late 1960s but fell out of love with it quite soon, for it was horridly loud and kicked like a mule. So I traded it in on the next item below.

Smith & Wesson .38-caliber revolver, Model 36 (short-barreled "Chief's Special") Acquired (again why?) in the swap mentioned above. I used this cylinder .38 very little except for occasional practice shooting and maybe a rattlesnake or two.

Browning .25-caliber semi-automatic. In 1964 I was invited along on a canoe float down the Conchos River in northern Mexico by the trip's organizer, Rodman Saville of Houston. No one seemed to know much about that river and there were no decent maps, nor any records we could find of previous voyages on it, but we headed out. Six of us put our three canoes and our gear and ourselves onto a freight train at Ojinaga, where the Conchos flows into the Rio Grande, and unloaded about a hundred miles upstream at a river town called Falomir Márques. And from Falomir we ran downstream for a few days through deserts and canyons to Ojinaga again.

Invading any remote part of Mexico was and still is a bit iffy in terms of what sorts of human beings one might encounter, so Rodman and I each brought along one of these tiny Brownings, an easily concealed if, in Mexico, illegal means of self-defense. Both of us were military veterans and knew that such miniature armament wouldn't stop any villains in their tracks unless they were hit in the head. But the things could be hidden in our smallest pockets and could if produced, we hoped, cause said villains to think twice before initiating violence.

As it turned out, we got along fine with the sparse and primitive population along the river's shores, in part because my Spanish was still fairly decent from living in Spain in the 1950s. This was true at least until we reached the always restless and, yes, dangerous zone near the Rio Grande, where smiles and waved hands became less prevalent than scowls as six unshaven, trip-soiled gringos paddled past in their chalupas.

There was no actual trouble, though I think we once came close to it in a canyon near the journey's end, where three unprepossessing characters in a wooden skiff paddled out to intercept us. They had a Winchester lever-action deer rifle propped against the boat's gunwale. None was smiling, and the musta-chioed largest one of them, sitting beside the rifle, asked what we were doing there. I told him. He was briefly silent, then said they were fishing and needed bait, and I told him that we had none. He studied us for a time, but if he had any action in mind he apparently decided there were too many of us. In silence he sig-naled the others to paddle back toward shore, and with relief we watched them go.

Later, Rodman and I compared notes and neither of us had had his little Browning where it could be reached in a hurry. So much for self-defense.

This diminutive threat has been called "the ladies' pistol," and I'm sure they have been utilized in a few serious marital scraps and murders, perhaps in the nickel-plated, pearl-handled version.

Ruger .22-caliber semi-auto, Mark II. I bought this one in the 1980s when Jane and I were driving to Key West each spring to fish with her brother John Cole, who was living there with his wife Jean. We had our own skiff that I had fixed up for such fishing, and would tow it down there on its trailer. The lower Keys were not as heavily frequented at that time as they would be within only a few years, and we were often alone among the many mangrove islets of the "back country" on the Gulf side, where there was much beauty and good fishing but also where dubious-looking Cubans or uncongenial poor-white Conch types sometimes turned up in boats.

We never had any trouble there except once when our pickup was ransacked at an isolated boat ramp where we had launched, but I believe in being prepared and this pistol, made of stainless steel because of the salt spray, was my instrument of preparedness.

It was a beauty, but I have a sometimes ill-advised habit of tinkering with new acquisitions, and I tinkered a bit too much with this one. It was shooting consistently lower than the points at which I aimed it, so I took a file and worked the front sight down to rectify this. I filed it a bit overmuch, though, and afterward the pistol shot too high. I became fully aware of this one weekend when we had a group of friends down here at our country place, with several children among them. Our creek was running nicely, so much of the activity was down by its little waterfall and the pool below. However, two separate good-sized rattlesnakes liked it down there too. I don't usually kill them unless they're where people are, but these most certainly were. I dispatched the first one with a stick, then brought this .22 from the pickup, whereupon the kids found another rattler far back under some bushes. I crouched down and started shooting at its head, but kept missing before I remembered the filed-down sight. One boy, the grandson of an old friend, then seven or eight years old, was right behind me as I fired, and with every shot he would yell "Kill him! Kill him!" until I finally did.

I had intended to replace that front sight, but as with many other things these days, I never got around to it.

Shotguns

Winchester Model 97 pump (slide-action) 12-gauge. The other antique from Cuero, older I think than Grandpa's little .32 automatic. "Model 97" means the type was first made in 1897, I'm sure, and this must have been an early specimen. According to the story Papa told me, in days before there were many game laws the gun had first belonged to a market duck- hunter. Those people were not sportsmen but ambushed their quarry on the water, preferably when they were flocked up and a single cartridge could harvest a good number of dead birds to sell. He in turn, probably after game laws got stiffer, sold or traded it to my father's older brother Will, who died in the Spanish flu epidemic in 1918, after which I assume it passed to Papa, though at some point it was used by Will's and Papa's younger brother Tommy. Tommy was the most avid hunter in the family, an excellent shot who also had great skill in blowing off the ends of shotgun barrels when they had been carelessly poked into dirt or mud. And he did this to the Model 97.

Parenthetically though without parentheses, I will note that along the way I inherited two other shotguns that Uncle Tommy had shortened in this fashion, both with double barrels of old-fashioned laminated Damascus steel, a handsome metal but intended for black-powder shells and too tender for safe use with modern smokeless ammunition, which Tommy may well have tried to fire in them. One of these Damascus doubles was a Baker 16-gauge with a single trigger, automatic extractors, and handsome woodwork, a real old beauty. For some odd reason, this Baker, which I never fired, later called to my mind the antiquated English muzzle-loader used by Caroline Gordon's title figure in her wonderful *Aleck Maury, Sportsman*, who is modeled on her own father.

At any rate, after Uncle Tommy had thus reduced the old Model 97, Papa—I think it was he—had a new 30-inch, full-choke, proof-steel barrel put on it, and this was the only shotgun he owned or fired for the rest of his less and less active hunting career. He used it even on quail, whose explosive flight when flushed from the grass is best dealt with by shorter barrels and more open chokes that give the small pellets required in that hunting a much wider pattern. But he was still a good shot and didn't do badly with it.

Not ever having been much of a duck hunter, I have only rarely fired this weapon, though it's still in good shape and at times during my family's latter-day rural life in relative isolation, it has been a comfort to own, leaning in a closet corner and loaded with double-ought buckshot shells against the possibility of evil intruders. It would just about blow a man in half. And it has occasionally been handy against predators, as I will note further along.

Remington Model 870 pump, 20-gauge. My uncle-by-marriage Shelley Tarkington, an Aggie and a First World War aviator, then a cotton broker till the 1929 crash, and finally the longtime postmaster in Cuero, was a passionately active hunter and bird-dog man who like most of his contemporaries had always used a 12-gauge gun. But as he aged and developed heart problems, his doctor persuaded him to change to a lighter piece, so he bought this one, which had interchangeable choke tubes that could be attached to its muzzle and was thus adaptable to several sorts of hunting. He was an even better shot than Uncle Tommy. I remember an occasion late in Shelley's life when he and

I went out after doves that were watering in the evenings at a cattle pond, a "tank." He had been warned against too much exercise, so he took shots only at incoming birds which, if hit, would fall close by. And with this gun he hardly missed a one, dropping them within a few feet of where he stood, so that he reached the legal limit of fifteen while I was still trying to kill my seventh or eighth bird.

To digress a bit, as seems to be getting usual in this document, Uncle Tommy also had to adjust his weaponry when older, though he didn't last nearly as long as Shelley did. One evening when he was in his late thirties or early forties, he was driving along a country road with his left elbow poking out of the car's open window. A large truck going in the opposite direction swerved as it passed (or maybe Tommy swerved— he sometimes drank a bit much) and sideswiped the car, shearing his arm off not far below the shoulder. After it had healed to a stub he refused to give up hunting, and got hold of a beautiful light 28-gauge double that he could handle with only his remaining arm, shooting nearly as well as he had with a 12-gauge and two arms.

Somehow appropriately, when he died of a massive heart attack at I think forty-seven, it followed a strenuous afternoon spent following his dogs after quail.

Another Tommy tale: once when he and I and Papa and Shelley were hunting together, Tommy brought along a setter named Chiefie, which had a fine nose and held firmly still on a point, but also had a bad habit of jumping into the air after birds when they were flushed. He never caught one that I know of, but he kept on doing this despite scoldings and castigation. On this day he found and pointed a covey in a patch of live oak brush and was backed up by Shelley's dog. They held beautifully as we moved in with guns at the ready, then flushed the covey when given the word. The quail exploded and all four of us started shooting, but the bird Tommy chose was in mid-flock and just as he fired, a leaping black head rose into line with the bird and the shotgun's pellets.

Without even a yelp, Chiefie fell limp to the ground. Shelley was the closest hunter and went over to look at the dog and feel various spots on its skull and throat.

He shook his head and said, "Gone!"

Tommy came up and did his own examining, and concurred. He said, "Nita's going to kill me. He was her favorite one of my dogs."

We put the corpse into our nearby car and kept on hunting with Shelley's pooch and another dog, a spare, released from its box in the car's trunk. We found more coveys and did well with them, but there was not great joy among us.

Two or three hours later the dogs led us back near the area of the accident and found some scattered single birds and pairs. One of us shot, and a muffled frantic barking came from the car, where Chiefie was springing up and down and clawing at the windowglass, eager to be back in the action. When set free, he ran in circles with joy, blood-flecked as he was, and hunted avidly for the rest of the day and the rest of his life. But Uncle Tommy told me later that Chiefie never again jumped up at a covey rise.

Shelley's Remington pump was given to me by Aunt Sally after he died in 1962, and I have used it for my own infrequent hunting ever since. The shotgun I had grown up with, an inexpensive double-barreled 20-gauge Springfield that had been a present on my twelfth Christmas, I gave to my nephew Robert Wynne, who was having trouble with rabbits in his vineyard in New Zealand.

In fact, I have now given away most of the guns in this list to younger relatives and friends, retaining only three or four for practical or sentimental reasons. These survivors include Shelley's pump, despite the fact that I still like doubles best, and for a good many years hoped I would end up with a really nice one—not a costly "bespoke" English Purdey or Holland and Holland, built to order after elaborate personal measurings and test-firings, but possibly an old but sound Parker, Ithaca, Fox, or L. C. Smith.

However doubles, old or new, grew steadily more pricey during an era when marriage and fatherhood and other expenses were chewing up my spending money. I do, however, still regret not buying a premium 16-gauge Winchester Model 21 with two sets of barrels, which a broke Air Force pilot once offered to me for $350. Regret it, even though at this point I'm not physically up to any more hunting at all.

Rifles

Winchester Model 06 pump .22. A holdover from childhood, given to me on my tenth birthday. This model, when chambered only for .22 "shorts," the least powerful cartridges in that caliber, was the standard at shooting galleries and carnival booths in those times, but a good many, like this one, were made for kids, short-stocked and chambered to accept all three types of .22 cartridges—shorts, longs, and long-rifles. I have cherished it all my life, and after World War Two I went to a good bit of trouble carving an adult-sized cherrywood stock and forearm for it, a pretty good job except for some bobbles in the checkering.

Back then youngsters were mainly introduced to firearms much earlier in life than I think most are today. You went from a BB airgun to a .22 more or less routinely, though a good bit of supervision was usually exercised. When he gave me this little rifle my father went out with me to try it on some targets and tin cans, and he told me, "You must never, never point this gun at anybody!" And I said, "No, Papa, I won't."

But two or three weeks later I was lying on my bed by a window, cherishing and polishing my new treasure, when a particular neighborhood enemy of mine came walking down a driveway next door. The rifle was not loaded, and I swung it to fix the sights on his head as he moved along, at which moment Papa walked into the room.

I didn't get the little .22 back for months, and even then it was with stern restrictions that involved getting permission to even touch it where it reposed in my parents' closet. Three or four years later, however, an ingenious neighbor boy evolved a method of replacing lead .22 bullets with candle wax, which we would then shoot at each other, and I don't remember Papa objecting to this. Or maybe he didn't know about it. At any rate, since that wax-bullet phase I have remained aware of his instructions all my life, and have never pointed a firearm purposely at any person except during the Pacific war.

This rifle, which has reaped a large harvest of rabbits and squirrels and varmints through the years, has also figured in certain small human dramas, a couple of which may be worth setting down here.

In the 1970s on our country property, a two-story east addition to our house was going up, and during one summer I was being helped in its construction by Jane's nephew Charlie Cole from Connecticut and a couple of friends' sons, Suter Dubose and Jim McBride of Fort Worth. Charlie and Suter were alone in the living room one day after lunch. Through my stupidity the little .22, loaded but without a shell in the chamber, was leaning in a corner, and Charlie, who knew nothing at all about guns, picked it up and aimed it at various points in the room, including Suter, while saying "Pow! Pow!" to emulate shots. Then he pumped the slide handle and pulled the trigger, and the resulting explosion sent a small hunk of lead through the polished front drawer of a handsome vintage secretary that Jane prized.

At least, I reflected afterward, it hadn't been Suter . . .

That hole is still with us, at Jane's insistence, as a part of family lore.

I seem, however, to have only partly learned from that incident what I should have learned about modern youngsters and guns. Not long afterward, when the addition had been framed and roofed but not finished inside and my helpers were back at their desks in school, we had a weekend visit from Bob and Laura Wilson of Dallas, with two of their young sons, who are both now well-known Hollywood actors. We adults were sitting in lawn chairs on the porch while the small Wilsons, eight or nine years old, were loudly exploring their environs and the unfinished construction.

Before they came I had put the little rifle, still loaded for possible snakes and varmints, but with an empty chamber, athwart the ceiling beams of what was to be our master bedroom, nearly nine feet above the floor. I was certain this would keep it out of the small Wilsons' reach, but I was dead wrong. It couldn't have been more than twenty minutes before one of the little devils raced past us on the porch, brandishing the rifle and emitting cowboy yells. He was furious when I chased him down and grabbed it away from him.

I still have the old .22, but it stays empty these days, with its ammunition stowed elsewhere.

Springfield 1873, .45-70-caliber, "trapdoor" single-shot action. Another Cuero relic, bought there by some relative as war surplus after the Spanish-American conflict, in which some of this model had still been used. It was too long and heavy for a kid to handle, and I had no .45-70 cartridges. I did find out that it would take .410 shotgun shells and "leaded up" its rifling by firing a few of them in it. Papa finally gave to a doctor, a gun-collecting friend, and I was not sad to see it go.

Remington Model 660 bolt-action, .243 Winchester caliber. During a long spell of years I put much work and energy into this country place where Jane and I still live, developing it as a stock farm. Its primary livestock were Angus or crossbred cattle, but we also needed goats to eat brush and keep it from reinfesting cleared land. At one time, in addition to a few pet Nubians kept in pens near our house, we had a herd of ninety or more "Spanish" or common goats, which roamed widely.

Small kid goats are easy meat for almost all wild carnivores, and need to be guarded against predation. But the schedule of goat reproduction usually means that kids are nearly all born at about the same time, so with care you can pen them for protection until they're larger and more agile, letting the nannies in from time to time to give the little ones milk and attention.

I guess I'd better put most of this into the past tense, since we no longer have any goats or the troubles associated with them. But those troubles are still fresh in my mind.

Mature goats and half-grown kids had only two main enemies in our region, and these were dogs and coyotes. The latter killed only what they could eat, and were so smart and cautious that after you had shot one or two of them they either moved elsewhere or stopped bothering your flock.

Dogs, though, were neither as bright nor as frugal in their depredations. There is mention of this problem early in Part One of this book, the "Blue" section, but it can stand a little further discussion. Mainly these marauding canines were referred to in rural regions as "wild" dogs so that dealing with them as they needed to be dealt with would not seem to involve killing people's pets, as it often did. For domestic dogs in the country, allowed to run free at night after perhaps playing with a family's children all day, would often gang up and traverse the landscape, slaughtering poultry, goats, sheep, and even small calves whose cow mothers were not pretty tough. All of this just for fun, not food. And when you had heard those dogs' barking and baying and snarling at midnight, and you went up a hill in the morning to find seven or eight or more goats dead, or dying with their guts hanging out, you tended to come back down with a much less sentimental view of dogs as a species, despite the carefully controlled ones you had at home.

That was why I bought this flat-shooting .243 and put a scope sight on it. With the old Model 97 12-gauge and its buckshot, the rifle saw good use on occasion, which I will not detail here except to note that it involved a bit of vengeful mayhem.

The .243 was also an efficient weapon for medium-large game, and when we were all living here as a family I used it to harvest some venison each year, even though I'd never been a dedicated deer-hunter and in fact didn't much like to kill them.

Miscellaneous items

Savage over-and-under combination .22 rifle and .410 shotgun. A piece of junk really, with no serial number and its two barrels poorly aligned so that their loads hit in different places. This one I bought for Jane when we were still living on that honkytonk western edge of west Fort Worth, and I told her, "If I'm not here and you think you hear somebody outside at night, just go out on the porch and shoot the shotgun barrel in the air and yell, 'I know you're there!'"

But she hates guns and I'm sure she never did this.

I didn't give up trying to interest her, however, not for a while. In the late 1960s, down at our own country place with its then-minimal living quarters, she and I were sitting in the main room one day when I brought out this ugly but very simple weapon to try once more to teach her how it worked.

"You get that?" I asked after putting a .22 cartridge into its chamber and snapping the barrels down into position. She said yes and I handed it to her. "Now unload it," I told her.

I did have the sense to give it to her pointed upward. She took it, pulled the hammer back, yanked the trigger, and shot a hole in the ceiling which is still there, unfilled for the same reason the hole in her heirloom secretary remains open. Family history.

That was about the end of my efforts to make Jane like guns.

Sheridan 5-mm pellet air rifle. In the late 1960s or early seventies, when we still had horses here that ate oats and scattered a lot of them around, we attracted a large infestation of English or "house" sparrows, a species that had burgeoned in their homeland when horses were primary in farming, commerce, sport, and travel. Our line of old, large live oaks in front of the house had not yet been devastated by the fungal blight that would kill them all a few years later, and those trees became a primary nesting and roosting area for the small invaders, which chased away more desirable birds and kept up an incessant chatter and a rain of droppings. I asked an ornithological acquaintance what to do about this. He said that unfortunately the only way he knew to control them was to kill as many as possible, which sooner or later would cause the survivors to go somewhere else. So on the advice of a gun-wise friend I bought this compact and accurate rifle and had it equipped with a peep-sight.

The gun was not a repeater and had to be pumped up after each shot to restore air pressure, but it worked extremely well. I would sit in a lawn chair beneath one of the oaks with my Australian heeler Blue beside me, and whenever a sparrow exposed itself in the foliage I would raise the pellet rifle and shoot. My eyesight was much better back then than it is now, so that with the peep-sight I only occasionally missed. As each victim fell to the ground, Blue would dash over and eat it, never seeming to get sick from the feathers.

With a hunting dog this would have been a very poor procedure, for those dogs are supposed to deliver downed quarry intact to the shooter. But Blue was purely a herder, not a hunter, and I fear we both came to enjoy the game, deadly as it was for the sparrows. It lasted for only a few weeks, though, before my ornithological friend was proved right and every single English sparrow on the place departed for realms unknown.

Blue's abrupt and mystifying disappearance one night in 1976 has been noted in Part One. It was years later before I came to believe, from something a local countryman told me, that he had probably been mistakenly killed by fur-hunters who then guiltily hauled the body away. The pelts of coons, ringtails, bobcats, foxes, and coyotes had been bringing premium prices back then, and these people simply stationed themselves in open areas like our fields across the creek, sounding an irresistible distressed-rabbit call, swiveling a spotlight around, and shooting through telescopic sights at the glowing eyes of any creature that showed up. And Blue, my informant believed, had been one of those.

I was even given a name for the surmised killer, but the fellow inconveniently suffered a fatal heart attack before I could work out some form of belated confrontation or revenge.

The shaggy Old English pup that replaced Blue was given to us by a friend who knew about our loss. Our girls dubbed him Hup, from a Booth cartoon, and he grew into a delightful dog, quick to learn and eager to please.

Hup's breed are headers rather than heelers, and a header's instinct is to get on the far side of livestock being worked and bring them back toward its master. Before I figured this out, it led to some ludicrous situations when I was trying to drive cows or goats or a neighbor's trespassing hogs into a corral or through a gate and Hup would race out in front of them and try to drive them back.

He lacked Blue's aggressive talent with varmints, but was more trainable in other activities, because less nervous. And, unexpectedly for a herding dog, he had a good nose and turned out to be an instinctive and excellent retriever of the doves, quail, and ducks I was still hunting at that time. He was "soft-mouthed," and brought shot birds back to drop them at my feet in good shape.

He was not perfect but then who is, canine of human? Once I took him along to hunt quail with a tolerant friend who had setters. I kept Hup at heel except when the time came for retrieval, at which he was more willing and capable than the bird dogs. At dusk we quit with ten or twelve quail each, and when leaving I put Hup in the bed of the pickup and tossed my game-bag after him.

Arriving at home, I let him out and took up the bag, which seemed strangely light. When I looked in, it contained exactly two birds, and Hup on the ground was watching me with what was clearly guilt in his eyes. His stomach when I felt it was swollen and tight. I started to scold him and he dropped his hairy head, but he looked so comically rueful that I couldn't help laughing and spoiling my angry pose. What I decided, still laughing, was just never to give him another shot at that particular sin. This may not have been necessary, though, for his bellyfull of meat and feathers and bones and entrails made him retchingly sick before bedtime, and this experience, coupled perhaps with shame, kept him ever afterward from wanting to eat any kind of birds at all, except maybe cooked chicken scraps.

There came an autumn when I had an eight or ten-acre field of ripe wheat that I hadn't been able to get harvested, so that by October it was a disorderly mess full of crisscrossed grain-laden stalks. But it was also a magnet for doves, which came there in hundreds, day after day. This was too much of a bonanza for one lone occasional sportsman, so I called a longtime hunting buddy in Fort Worth, who brought six or seven other friends down to the place. One of these I had been close to since our first grade in school. He was not a happy hunter, maybe because of wartime experiences, so he and I stayed talking on high ground from which we could watch the melee in the field below.

The shooting there was constant, and so, quite soon, were the shouts of "Hup! Hup! Over here, Hup!" because the shot birds that fell into the tangled wheat or the brush bordering the field were very hard for human eyes to discern. But every shooter "limited out" and lost not a bird, all because of the nose, skill, and eagerness of a dog that was not supposed to be a retriever at all.

However, Hup was out of dog-show stock (his sire had been a champion), with systemic defects brought on by inbreeding. He lasted only to the age of six before collapsing miserably with a combination of dysplasia, pancreatitis, and constant diarrhea, so that sadly I had to have the vet "put him to sleep," as the euphemism has it.

Not long before Hup broke down, however, I had bred him to a far less patrician Old English bitch belonging to a local lady, and later had given the breeding fee—my choice among the resulting pups—to a friend. When the friend heard that I had lost Hup, he insisted that I take the pup back, and this was Hodge.

Hodge was much like his sire in a number of ways, though not as anxious to please or as amenable to training. He too was a header, but a fierce and noisy one who could panic livestock and wreck a drive. So I had to put him on a leash or leave him at the house when engaging in such work. He had Hup's good nose and loved retrieving shot birds, but often dashed out when doves, say, were flying in, and scared them out of range. When I did shoot one, he would find it and bring it in, but would usually chomp on it all the way, so that what he presented me with was a gory bunch of feathers.

For these reasons I seldom took him along when I was hunting with friends, but he gentled with time and we became quite close, as men and their dogs usually do. With his plebeian genes, he lasted thirteen years, and during the last three or four of them, having been bawled out and punished time and again for that chomping, he gave it up, but without developing a soft mouth. Instead of bringing a downed bird back to me, he would go out and stand with his nose pointing down at it, finding every one, and would wait for me to limp out on arthritic legs to pick it up. On one occasion a dove was only winged and fluttered a few yards farther out each time Hodge moved up and stood over it again. As I trudged toward him I could see him puzzling over the problem, and finally he put his paw on the bird, holding it in place till I came.

No, when Hodge died I didn't have a younger replacement on hand as I resolved I would in the "Blue" chapter. I find that age does away with many earlier resolutions, and I'm no longer up to the herding and hunting and other outdoor action that could justify owning the sort of dogs that have meant so much to me in years past. I still cherish remembering them, though.

Thus, in these observations, we have strayed from dogs to guns, then back to dogs again. I myself don't mind this and I hope my preferred sort of readers won't mind it either. Although firearms and working dogs and hunting and so on are increasingly old-fashioned and unpopular subjects in a time when a heavily urban public seeks "virtual" experience through electronics and is increasingly sentimental about wild creatures including those that have long been viewed as "game," I myself remain pretty much an unrepentant anachronism, if a somewhat battered one. But there are still a good many of us around, and I hope this little book will find its path to the eyes of some thinkers among them.

Therefore so long, all you fellow anachronisms out there.